W9-DDN-421

CRANES
LIFT!

by Beth Bence Reinke

BUMBA BOOKS™

LERNER PUBLICATIONS ◆ MINNEAPOLIS

Note to Educators:

Throughout this book, you'll find critical thinking questions. These can be used to engage young readers in thinking critically about the topic and in using the text and photos to do so.

Lerner Publications Company
A division of Lerner Publishing Group, Inc.
241 First Avenue North
Minneapolis, MN 55401 USA

For reading levels and more information, look up this title at www.lernerbooks.com.

Library of Congress Cataloging-in-Publication Data

The Cataloging-in-Publication Data for *Cranes Lift!* is on file at the Library of Congress.
ISBN 978-1-5124-3356-2 (lib. bdg.)
ISBN 978-1-5124-5542-7 (pbk.)
ISBN 978-1-5124-5022-4 (EB pdf)

Manufactured in the United States of America
1—CG—7/15/17

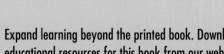

Expand learning beyond the printed book. Download free, complementary educational resources for this book from our website, www.lerneresource.com.

Table of
Contents

Cranes

Cranes work at construction sites.

They lift loads.

They reach high in the air.

Why do cranes need to lift high in the air?

The crane operator sits in the

crane's cab.

He controls the long arm.

A strong wire hangs from the arm.

The wire is called a cable.

A big hook at the end

of the cable holds the load.

The arm goes up.

The cable goes up.

They lift a steel beam.

The crane sets the beam in place.

What do you think cranes help build?

Some cranes are built

on trucks.

These cranes drive

to each job.

This crane has tracks.

Tracks help it move on the

bumpy ground.

Where might cranes with tracks work best?

tracks

15

A tower crane is very tall.

The long arm on the tower

crane is called a jib.

Tower cranes build tall buildings.

They lift supplies to the very top.

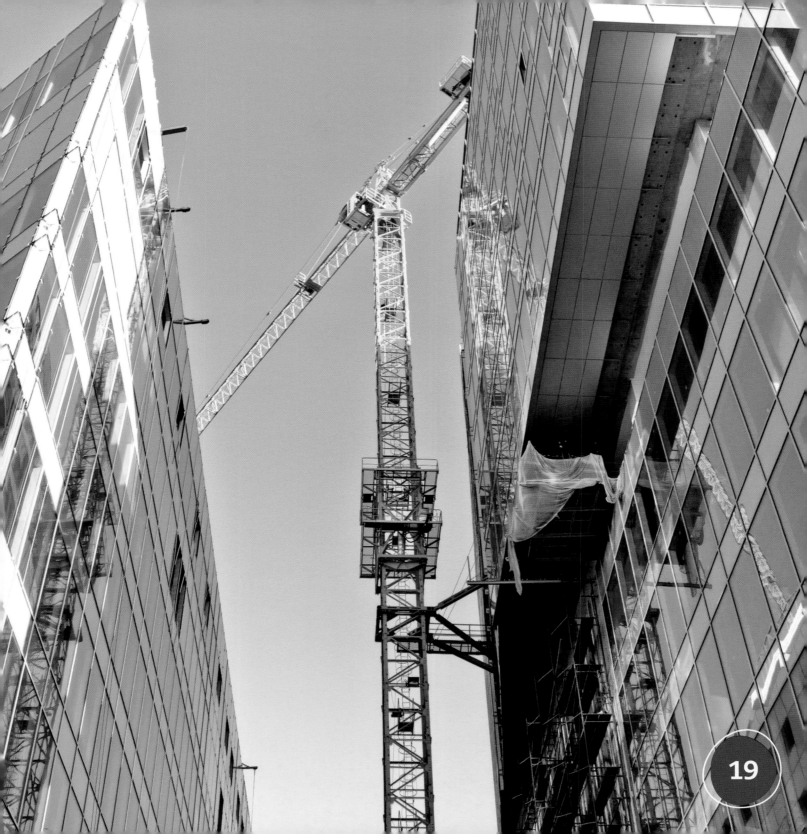

Cranes lift things

with their long arms.

They help do jobs

in high places.

Parts of a Crane

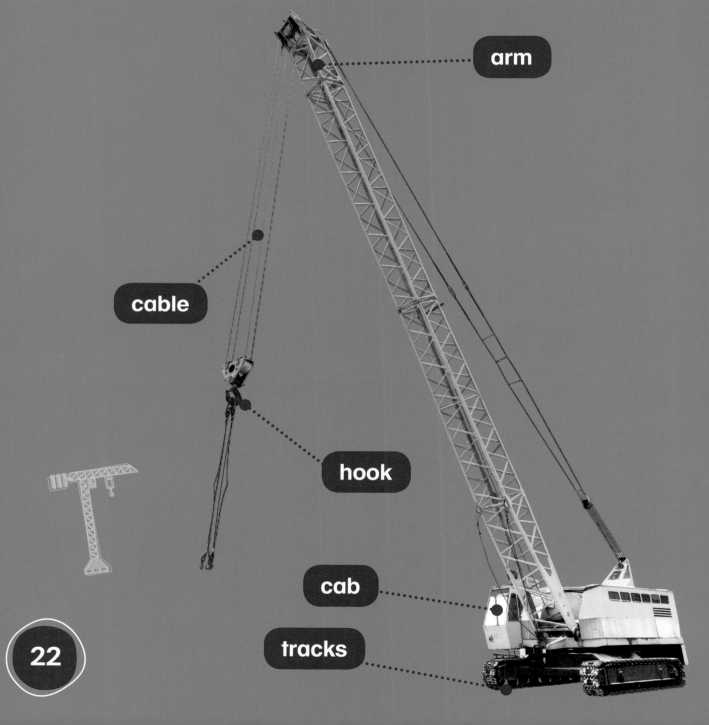

arm

cable

hook

cab

tracks

Picture Glossary

beam

a long and heavy piece of metal or wood that is used to support a building

construction sites

places where construction, or building, takes place

operator

the person who controls the crane

tracks

belts that move a crane over the ground

Read More

Dieker, Wendy Strobel. *Cranes*. Minneapolis: Bullfrog Books, 2013.

Osier, Dan. *Cranes*. New York: PowerKids, 2014.

Reinke, Beth Bence. *Bulldozers Push!* Minneapolis: Lerner Publications, 2018.

Index

Photo Credits